YELLOWSTONE NATIONAL PARK TRAVEL GUIDE 2025

Discover Best Hikes, Scenic Drives, Wildlife Spotting, Camping Tips, and Road Trip Itineraries for an Unforgettable Adventure

Albert N. Allred

Copyright © 2025 (Albert N.Allred)

All rights reserved. No part of this book may be reproduced or transmitted in any form or by any means, electronic or mechanical, including photocopying, recording or by any information storage and retrieval system, without written permission from the author, except for the inclusion of brief quotations embodied in critical reviews and certain other non commercial uses permitted by copyright law.

DISCLAIMER

Welcome to the **Yellowstone National Park Travel Guide 2025!** This guide is designed to help you explore the wonders of Yellowstone, from its iconic geothermal features to its diverse wildlife and stunning landscapes.

Notice: While every effort has been made to provide accurate and up-to-date information, please be aware that conditions within the park—including trail status, seasonal access, operating hours, and local services—may change. We recommend confirming details with official Yellowstone resources, park rangers, or service providers for the most current information prior to your visit. Stay informed, stay safe, and enjoy your Yellowstone adventure!

Table Of Contents

Introduction..................................7

Chapter 1: Getting to Know Yellowstone 9
    A. A Brief History   9
    B. Yellowstone Geology   12
    C. How To Use This Guide   14

Chapter 2: Itinerary Planning   17
    A. Best Times To Visit   17
    B. Suggested Itineraries   19

Chapter 3: Transportation Options   25
    A. Getting There   25
    B. Getting Around   29

Chapter 4: Yellowstone's Natural Wonders...   33
    A. The Geothermal Features   33
    B. Iconic Geothermal Sites   37
    C. Yellowstone Lake and Its Scenic Beauty   43
    D. Yellowstone's Rivers and Waterfalls 46

Chapter 5: Outdoor Activities   51
    A. Hiking Trails for all Levels   51
    B. Backpacking Routes and Overnight Trips   53

    C. Boating, Fishing, and Water Sports 55

Chapter 6: Wildlife Encounters 59
    A. The Big Five 59
    B. Best Places for Wildlife Viewing 60
    C. How to Safely Observe Wildlife 61
    D. Bird Watching in Yellowstone 61

Chapter 7: Where to Stay in Yellowstone 63
    A. Lodgings Inside The Park 63
    B. Camping In Yellowstone 65

Chapter 8: Dining and Shopping 69
    A. Best Restaurants and Dining Spots in the Park 69
    B. Picnic Areas and Outdoor Dining 74
    C. Must-Try Local Cuisine and Snacks 75
    D. Shopping for Souvenirs and Unique Gifts 76

Chapter 9: Yellowstone Beyond the Park 79
    A. Day Trips Near Yellowstone 79
    B. Local Culture 84
    C. Visiting Native American Sites and Learning About Local Tribes 91

Chapter 10: Safety, Travel Tips, and Park Etiquette 97

A. Health and Emergency Services in the Park   97
B. What to Pack for Your Yellowstone Adventure   98
C. Cell Service, Wi-Fi, and Communication While in the Park   100
D. Park Etiquette   101

Conclusion   103

Yellowstone National Park

Introduction

Welcome to *Yellowstone National Park Travel Guide 2025*, where adventure, awe, and natural wonders await at every turn! If you've ever dreamed of exploring the heart of America's first national park, this guide is your ultimate companion. From its world-famous geothermal wonders to its stunning landscapes, abundant wildlife, and the ever-present sense of discovery, Yellowstone holds a magical allure that draws visitors from around the globe.

Every time I set foot in Yellowstone, it feels like a love affair that deepens with each visit. The park's majestic beauty never fails to take my breath away, whether it's witnessing the explosive power of Old Faithful, encountering bison roaming freely across vast plains, or simply gazing at the glistening waters of Yellowstone Lake as the sun sets.

In this guide, we'll take you on a journey through Yellowstone's unforgettable experiences, uncovering hidden gems and exploring must-see destinations. But it's not just about the sights—it's about the stories. The history, the geology, and the profound connection between humans and this incredible wilderness. Whether you're hiking through verdant forests, soaking in natural hot springs, or photographing wildlife, Yellowstone offers a life-changing experience that stays with you long after you've left.

So, grab your gear, pack your sense of adventure, and get ready to explore one of the most iconic and inspiring places on earth. Yellowstone isn't just a destination; it's a journey into the wild heart of nature, and 2025 is the perfect time to discover it for yourself. Let's dive in—your adventure starts now!

Chapter 1: Getting to Know Yellowstone

A. A Brief History

Yellowstone National Park holds a special place in the hearts of nature lovers and adventurers alike. As the first national park in the world, it is not just a place of stunning beauty, but also a symbol of the importance of preserving our natural treasures. The story of Yellowstone is rich with discovery, exploration, and vision, and it begins long before it became a protected area.

Before European settlers arrived, Yellowstone was home to Indigenous tribes for thousands of years. Native American tribes like the Crow, Shoshone, Blackfeet, and

Bannock lived in and around the park. They had a deep spiritual connection with the land, and many of the park's features, such as geysers and hot springs, were seen as sacred. They used the park's natural resources for food, medicine, and cultural practices. While the park may have been a place of mystery to early settlers, for these tribes, it was a familiar and revered landscape.

The first non-Native American to explore Yellowstone is believed to be John Colter, a member of the Lewis and Clark expedition. In the early 1800s, Colter ventured into what we now call Yellowstone and described strange sights like hot springs, bubbling mud pots, and geysers. His reports were so wild and outlandish that many believed he was simply telling tall tales. It wasn't until more explorers and scientists ventured into the area that the true wonders of Yellowstone began to be understood.

In 1869, a group of explorers led by the famous painter Thomas Moran and geologist Ferdinand Hayden made a major expedition into Yellowstone. Moran's beautiful paintings of the landscape and Hayden's scientific findings helped to convince the American public of the park's unique value. These images and reports of the geysers, waterfalls, and vast wilderness spread quickly, stirring people's imaginations. It became clear that Yellowstone was a place unlike any other, deserving of protection and preservation.

However, it wasn't until 1872 that Yellowstone truly became a protected area. President Ulysses S. Grant signed a bill that established Yellowstone as the world's first national park. The idea behind this groundbreaking decision was simple: preserve the park's natural beauty for future generations to enjoy, ensuring that its geothermal wonders, wildlife, and untouched landscapes would remain untouched by development. This was a radical idea at the time, as the concept of national parks was virtually unknown.

Since then, Yellowstone has faced its challenges. In its early years, the park struggled with poaching, over-hunting, and lack of resources. But slowly, the importance of protecting this place gained momentum. The establishment of the National Park Service in 1916 provided Yellowstone with the dedicated management it needed to thrive. Over the years, the park grew in both size and significance, and today it remains a cornerstone of America's natural heritage.

The park's history is also marked by the rise of scientific exploration. Researchers and park rangers have worked tirelessly to understand Yellowstone's complex geology, its volcanic origins, and the role it plays in ecosystems. The park sits atop a massive volcanic hot spot, and its geothermal activity continues to awe and inspire visitors from all over the world.

Yellowstone has also played a pivotal role in the conservation movement. Its vast wilderness has become a haven for wildlife, including bison, wolves, and grizzly bears, whose populations had once been decimated. The reintroduction of wolves in the 1990s was a particularly landmark moment, showing that conservation efforts can help restore balance to the natural world.

Today, Yellowstone continues to be a place of wonder, discovery, and reflection. It's a reminder of the power of nature and the importance of preserving our world's most precious landscapes. The history of Yellowstone is one of both human and natural resilience—a story that continues to unfold as visitors from around the world come to experience its magic.

B. Yellowstone Geology

Yellowstone's geology is one of the most fascinating and powerful aspects of the park. What makes this place so special is that it sits on top of one of the largest active volcanic systems in the world—a supervolcano. The land beneath your feet in Yellowstone holds the power of ancient and ongoing volcanic activity, shaping everything from the park's famous geysers to its stunning mountain ranges. But how did all of this come to be?

Millions of years ago, long before Yellowstone became a national park, the area was nothing like the peaceful wilderness we know today. The park sits on top of a giant volcanic hot spot. A "hot spot" is a place where hot material from deep within the Earth rises towards the surface, creating volcanic activity. Over the course of about 2 million years, the Yellowstone hot spot has caused three massive eruptions. These eruptions were so powerful that they shaped the entire landscape and created the caldera—the massive crater that defines Yellowstone's geological makeup.

The first eruption, about 2 million years ago, was so huge that it changed the landscape forever, creating a deep depression in the Earth's surface. This was the start of what we now call the Yellowstone Caldera. The second eruption, about 1.3 million years ago, was even larger. And the third, about 640,000 years ago, was one of the biggest eruptions in Earth's history. It left behind a huge, bowl-shaped depression that stretches about 30 miles wide—this is the caldera we see today.

While Yellowstone's volcano may not be as active as it was millions of years ago, it's still alive with geothermal activity. This hot spot continues to power the park's famous geothermal features—hot springs, geysers, mud pots, and fumaroles. These are all connected to the heat rising from deep within the Earth. The geothermal features in Yellowstone are a direct result of the volcanic activity that has been ongoing for millions of years.

Perhaps the most iconic feature of Yellowstone's geology is its geysers. Old Faithful, the most famous of them all, erupts regularly and spectacularly, shooting water and steam high into the air. But Old Faithful is just one of many geysers in Yellowstone. The park is home to over 500 geysers, making it the largest concentration of geysers in the world. These geysers are created when underground water comes into contact with the intense heat from the Earth's core, causing it to boil and shoot up to the surface.

Another fascinating aspect of Yellowstone's geology is its hot springs. These natural pools of hot water are formed when water from rain or snow seeps into the ground, where it's heated by the Earth's geothermal activity. As the water rises to the surface, it creates colorful, mineral-rich springs. The Grand Prismatic Spring, one of the largest and most beautiful hot springs in the world, is a perfect example. Its brilliant colors are caused by bacteria that thrive in the hot, mineral-rich waters.

Yellowstone is also home to fascinating mud pots—bubbling, steaming pools of thick, soupy mud—and fumaroles, which are vents in the Earth's crust that release steam and gases. All of these features are signs that the land beneath Yellowstone is still very much alive, constantly changing, and evolving.

C.How To Use This Guide

This guide is designed to be a helpful and easy-to-follow resource for making the most of your visit to Yellowstone National Park. Here are some important details on how to use it effectively:

1. **Explore Key Sections Based on Your Interests**
   - The guide is divided into chapters that focus on different aspects of the park, such as its history, geology, wildlife, activities, and lodging. Depending on your interests, you can dive directly into the sections that appeal to you the most, whether it's exploring wildlife viewing opportunities, planning your hiking routes, or understanding the park's geothermal features.
2. **Suggested Itineraries**
   - If you're unsure about how to structure your visit, this guide provides suggested itineraries based on different time frames (e.g., 2-day, 5-day, and 7-day options). These itineraries include recommended sights, activities, and routes, helping you make the most of your time in the park.
3. **Practical Travel Tips**
   - Throughout the guide, you'll find practical tips for navigating Yellowstone. From how to get there and where to stay to what to pack and how to stay safe, this section is filled with useful advice for a smooth trip.
4. **Wildlife Watching Guidelines**

- If you're planning to see Yellowstone's incredible wildlife, this guide includes sections on how to safely view animals like bison, wolves, and bears. It also covers the best times and places to spot wildlife, along with tips on respecting the animals and their habitats.

5. **Geothermal Features**
    - Yellowstone is known for its geothermal wonders, and this guide helps you explore them in-depth. From geysers like Old Faithful to hot springs and mud pots, you'll find information on what to expect, when to visit, and how to appreciate the beauty and science behind these natural wonders.

6. **Lodging and Dining Options**
    - The guide provides recommendations for a range of accommodation options within and around the park, from camping to more luxurious stays. Additionally, you'll find dining suggestions, including restaurants, cafes, and places to pick up quick meals or snacks for your outdoor adventures.

7. **Activities and Adventures**
    - Whether you're interested in hiking, fishing, or simply soaking in the scenery, this guide outlines the best activities for all types of adventurers. It provides descriptions of trails, water-based activities, and wildlife encounters, ensuring you don't miss out on the park's top experiences.

Chapter 2: Itinerary Planning

A. Best Times To Visit

Choosing the best time to visit Yellowstone depends on what kind of experience you're seeking. Yellowstone is a year-round destination, but the park's seasons each offer distinct advantages.

- **Summer (June to August)**: This is the most popular time to visit, and for good reason. The weather is warm, with daytime temperatures ranging from 70°F to 80°F (21°C to 27°C), and most of the park's roads, accommodations, and services are open. Summer is ideal for hiking, wildlife watching, and exploring the park's

geothermal features. However, it also means the park can be crowded, especially in key areas like Old Faithful and the Grand Prismatic Spring. If you're planning a summer visit, be sure to book accommodations early.
- **Fall (September to October)**: If you prefer fewer crowds and cooler temperatures, fall is a great time to visit. Temperatures in fall can range from 30°F to 60°F (-1°C to 16°C), and the park begins to quiet down after the summer rush. Fall is also the best time to see the elk rutting season, where the bulls engage in impressive vocal battles to establish dominance. The autumn foliage adds an extra layer of beauty to Yellowstone's already stunning landscapes, especially around Yellowstone Lake and the Lamar Valley.
- **Winter (November to March)**: For those looking for a truly serene experience, winter offers a magical time to visit Yellowstone. Temperatures often drop below freezing, ranging from 5°F to 25°F (-15°C to -4°C), but the park's snowy landscapes and frozen geothermal features are truly breathtaking. Winter visitors can enjoy activities like snowshoeing, cross-country skiing, and snowmobile tours. Keep in mind that many of the park's facilities and roads close during the winter, so you'll need to plan accordingly. However, if you love winter wonderlands and solitude, this is the time for you.
- **Spring (April to May)**: Spring in Yellowstone brings a gradual thaw, with daytime temperatures ranging from 40°F to 60°F (4°C to 16°C). Snow starts to melt, and the wildlife begins to come alive. Spring is one of the best

times for spotting newborn animals, such as baby bison and elk. However, be prepared for muddy trails and cooler nights. Some roads and accommodations may still be closed until later in May, but this season offers a quieter, more peaceful experience than the summer months.

B. Suggested Itineraries

Whether you're visiting for a short trip or an extended stay, these suggested itineraries will help you make the most of your time in Yellowstone.

- **3-Day Itinerary**:
  - **Day 1**: Start your visit with a trip to the Upper Geyser Basin to see Old Faithful. Afterward, explore the nearby geothermal features like the Grand Prismatic Spring and Fountain Paint Pots. End the day with a wildlife drive through Hayden Valley.
  - **Day 2**: Head to the Lamar Valley for wildlife viewing in the morning. Afterward, explore the Grand Canyon of the Yellowstone, visiting the Lower Falls and Artist Point for stunning views. Finish your day with a visit to Yellowstone Lake.
  - **Day 3**: Spend your last day exploring the Mammoth Hot Springs Terraces and the surrounding area. Before leaving, stop by the Norris Geyser Basin and enjoy a short hike or a ranger-led tour.
- **5-Day Itinerary**:
  - **Day 1**: Explore Old Faithful and the surrounding geothermal features. Visit

the nearby Biscuit Basin and Midway Geyser Basin, home to the Grand Prismatic Spring.
  - **Day 2**: Visit the Grand Canyon of the Yellowstone, including both the Upper and Lower Falls, and take in panoramic views from Artist Point. In the afternoon, head to the Lamar Valley for some wildlife viewing.
  - **Day 3**: Take a scenic drive to Yellowstone Lake and enjoy a relaxing afternoon by the water. Consider a boat tour or fishing outing, if you're interested.
  - **Day 4**: Explore Mammoth Hot Springs and the surrounding historic district. Then, venture to Norris Geyser Basin to see Steamboat Geyser, the world's tallest active geyser.
  - **Day 5**: Spend the day hiking in the park's quieter areas, such as the Fairy Falls Trail or the Lamar River Trail, to enjoy some peace and quiet before leaving.
- **7-Day Itinerary**:
  - **Day 1**: Begin with Old Faithful and nearby geothermal areas. Spend the afternoon exploring Biscuit Basin and Midway Geyser Basin, taking plenty of time for photos and sightseeing.
  - **Day 2**: Head to the Grand Canyon of the Yellowstone for a day of hiking and taking in the views. Don't miss Uncle Tom's Trail for a close-up look at the Lower Falls.

- Day 3: Take a wildlife-focused day in the Lamar Valley and Hayden Valley, stopping at the Lamar River to see bison, wolves, and other wildlife.
- Day 4: Visit Yellowstone Lake, and consider a scenic boat tour or explore the West Thumb Geyser Basin.
- Day 5: Take a trip to Mammoth Hot Springs and explore the terraces and surrounding trails. Then, visit the historic Fort Yellowstone area.
- Day 6: Visit the Norris Geyser Basin and take a hike along the Porcelain Basin Trail to explore the area further.
- Day 7: Conclude your visit with a scenic drive through the park, stopping for a hike or to enjoy some of the park's quieter, lesser-known corners, such as the Lamar River Trail or the Slough Creek area.

Family Friendly Itineraries

Day 1: Exploring the Geysers and Waterfalls

- **Morning:** Start your adventure with a visit to **Old Faithful**. Watch this iconic geyser erupt, and explore the surrounding **Upper Geyser Basin**, where you can take a short and easy walk to see other fascinating geothermal features like **Castle Geyser** and **Fountain Paint Pots**.
- **Afternoon:** Head to the **Grand Canyon of the Yellowstone** to see the park's famous **Lower Falls**. The walk to **Artist Point** offers an incredible family-friendly view of the falls. You can also visit the **Canyon Visitor Education**

Center to learn about the park's geology and natural history, with interactive exhibits that kids will enjoy.
- **Evening**: Wind down with a relaxing evening at **Yellowstone Lake**, where families can enjoy a picnic by the water. There's also a chance to see the sunset over the lake and watch for wildlife, like bison and elk, in the area.

Day 2: Wildlife Viewing and Scenic Drives

- **Morning**: Start the day early with a drive through **Hayden Valley**, one of the best places in the park for wildlife viewing. You'll likely spot bison, elk, and possibly even wolves or bears. Kids will love spotting the animals from the safety of your car or from designated viewing areas.
- **Afternoon**: Take a short, easy hike on the **Lamar River Trail** or explore the **Mammoth Hot Springs** terraces. The boardwalks and accessible pathways make it easy for families with young children or strollers. The colorful terraces and bubbling springs are sure to captivate everyone.
- **Evening**: For a family-friendly dinner, head to the **Mammoth Hot Springs Hotel** or another park lodge to enjoy a casual meal. If time allows, take a stroll through the **historic Fort Yellowstone** area to learn about the park's past in a fun and educational way.

Day 3: A Day of Adventure and Relaxation

- **Morning**: Visit the **West Thumb Geyser Basin**, which is less crowded but equally fascinating. The boardwalks here provide a safe way to

explore the geothermal pools and springs. Afterward, enjoy a family-friendly boat ride on **Yellowstone Lake**. The boat tour offers a relaxing and scenic way to enjoy the park's beauty from the water.
- **Afternoon**: Head to **Norris Geyser Basin** and explore the **Porcelain Basin**. The boardwalks and shorter trails make it easy to take in the geothermal features without exhausting younger family members. Make sure to stop by the **Norris Visitor Center** for more hands-on exhibits and information about Yellowstone's geothermal activity.
- **Evening**: If the kids are up for it, consider a short evening walk at **Biscuit Basin** or **Fairy Falls** for a peaceful end to your day. Otherwise, enjoy a quiet evening at your accommodation, perhaps watching the sunset over the park's stunning landscapes.

Chapter 3: Transportation Options

A. Getting There

Planning your journey to Yellowstone National Park by air is both convenient and scenic. In 2025, several airports serve as gateways to this natural wonder, each offering unique advantages. Here's a guide to help you choose the best option for your visit.

1. Bozeman Yellowstone International Airport (BZN)

- **Location**: Belgrade, Montana, approximately 90 miles (about a 2-hour drive) from Yellowstone's North Entrance.
- **Description**: As Montana's busiest airport, BZN offers a wide range of domestic flights, especially during peak tourist seasons. The airport is well-equipped with amenities,

including rental car services, dining options, and free Wi-Fi.
- **Contact**: 850 Gallatin Field Rd, Belgrade, MT 59714. Phone: +1 406-388-8321.
- **Transportation to Yellowstone**: Upon arrival, you can rent a car or utilize shuttle services to reach the park. Notably, during the winter season, Yellowstone National Park Lodges offers a daily shuttle from BZN to Mammoth Hot Springs Hotel, providing a hassle-free transfer to the park.

2. Jackson Hole Airport (JAC)

- **Location**: Jackson, Wyoming, approximately 50 miles (about a 1-hour drive) from Yellowstone's South Entrance.
- **Description**: Nestled within Grand Teton National Park, JAC is the only airport located within a national park. It offers a unique arrival experience with stunning mountain views. The airport provides essential services, including rental car facilities and dining options.
- **Contact**: 1250 E Airport Rd, Jackson, WY 83001. Phone: +1 307-733-7690.
- **Transportation to Yellowstone**: From JAC, you can rent a car or join guided tours that offer transportation to Yellowstone. The drive to the South Entrance is scenic, passing through Grand Teton National Park.

3. Idaho Falls Regional Airport (IDA)

- **Location**: Idaho Falls, Idaho, approximately 110 miles (about a 2-hour drive) from Yellowstone's West Entrance.

- **Description**: IDA is a regional airport offering flights to and from major cities. While smaller than BZN, it provides essential services, including rental car agencies and a few dining options.
- **Contact**: 2140 N Skyline Dr, Idaho Falls, ID 83402. Phone: +1 208-528-6000.
- **Transportation to Yellowstone**: Car rentals are available at the airport. The drive to the West Entrance is straightforward, with scenic views along the way.

4. Yellowstone Regional Airport (COD)

- **Location**: Cody, Wyoming, approximately 53 miles (about a 1-hour drive) from Yellowstone's East Entrance.
- **Description**: COD is a smaller airport with limited commercial flights. It offers basic amenities, including rental car services.
- **Contact**: 2011 D Ave, Cody, WY 82414. Phone: +1 307-587-5110.
- **Transportation to Yellowstone**: Car rentals are available at the airport. The drive to the East Entrance is relatively short, making it a convenient option for visitors.

5. Billings Logan International Airport (BIL)

- **Location**: Billings, Montana, approximately 125 miles (about a 2-hour drive) from Yellowstone's Northeast Entrance.
- **Description**: BIL is Montana's largest airport, offering a variety of domestic flights. The airport is equipped with rental car services, dining options, and free Wi-Fi.

- **Contact**: 1901 Terminal Cir, Billings, MT 59105. Phone: +1 406-247-8609.
- **Transportation to Yellowstone**: Car rentals are available at the airport. The drive to the Northeast Entrance is scenic, passing through the Absaroka-Beartooth Wilderness.

Travel Tips:

- **Flight Booking**: During peak seasons (summer and early fall), flights to these airports can fill up quickly. It's advisable to book your flights well in advance to secure the best rates and preferred flight times.
- **Car Rentals**: All these airports offer car rental services. Given the expansive nature of Yellowstone, having a rental car provides flexibility and convenience. Ensure you have a valid driver's license and familiarize yourself with local driving laws.
- **Shuttle Services**: Some airports, like BZN, offer shuttle services to Yellowstone. These services can be convenient, especially if you prefer not to drive. Check with your accommodation to see if they offer shuttle services or can recommend reliable providers.
- **Seasonal Considerations**: Be aware of the seasonal operations of these airports. For instance, some airports may have limited services during the winter months. Always check the airport's official website or contact them directly for the most current information.

B. Getting Around

Exploring Yellowstone National Park is an adventure in itself, and understanding your transportation options is key to making the most of your visit. Here's a detailed guide to help you navigate the park in 2025:

By Car

Driving your own vehicle offers the freedom to explore at your own pace. The park's main attractions are connected by the Grand Loop Road, a figure-eight route that covers approximately 142 miles. This road is well-maintained, but be prepared for variable weather conditions, especially in spring and fall.

- **Road Conditions**: While most roads are open from late spring to early fall, some may close due to weather or construction. Always check the latest road conditions before your trip.
- **Parking**: Parking is available at major attractions, but spaces can fill up quickly during peak hours. Arriving early in the morning or

later in the evening can help you find parking more easily.
- **Fuel**: Gas stations are limited within the park. The largest service stations are located at Mammoth Hot Springs, West Yellowstone, and Canyon Village. Fuel prices are typically higher inside the park, so consider refueling before entering.

Car Rental Services and Rates

Renting a car provides flexibility and convenience for exploring Yellowstone. Here are some car rental services available near the park:

Avis Rent A Car: Located at Yellowstone Airport (WYS), Avis offers a range of vehicles, including SUVs and minivans, ideal for navigating the park's terrain.

Budget Rent A Car: Situated in West Yellowstone, Budget provides various car options, from compact cars to SUVs, catering to different travel needs.

Big Sky Car Rental: Offering a variety of vehicles, including compact cars, SUVs, and Jeeps, Big Sky Car Rentals is a convenient option for visitors.

Shuttle Services

If you prefer not to drive, several shuttle services operate within and around Yellowstone. These services can be particularly useful for reaching remote areas or during the winter months when some roads are closed to regular vehicles.

- **Winter Shuttle**: During the winter season, a daily shuttle operates between Bozeman

Yellowstone International Airport and Mammoth Hot Springs Hotel. This service is ideal for guests arriving during the winter months when many roads are closed to private vehicles. The shuttle departs at 12:45 pm and arrives at 4:00 pm. The cost is $107.78 for adults and $53.89 for children aged 3-11.
- **Tour Operators**: Various tour companies offer guided bus tours of the park, providing transportation to major attractions along with expert commentary. These tours can range from half-day excursions to multi-day adventures.

By Bike

Yellowstone offers a few designated bike trails, providing a unique way to experience the park's beauty. However, cycling on the main roads is challenging due to traffic and terrain.

- **Bike Trails**: The Yellowstone Lake area features some scenic biking routes, such as the Yellowstone Lake Loop. This trail is relatively flat and offers stunning views of the lake and surrounding mountains.
- **Guided Bike Tours**: For those interested in cycling without the hassle of planning, guided bike tours are available. These tours typically provide bikes and guides, allowing you to explore the park's beauty safely and informatively.

Winter Transportation

During the winter months, most roads in Yellowstone are closed to private vehicles. However, the park remains accessible through guided snowmobile and snow coach tours.

- **Snowcoaches**: These vehicles are designed for snowy conditions and offer a comfortable way to explore the park's winter landscapes. They typically operate between Mammoth Hot Springs and Old Faithful, providing access to major attractions even when roads are closed to regular vehicles. The cost for a snowcoach tour is approximately $160 for adults and $140 for children.
- **Snowmobile Tours**: For a more adventurous experience, guided snowmobile tours are available. These tours allow you to access areas of the park that are otherwise closed during the winter months. Note that snowmobile access is regulated to protect the park's resources, so tours are typically led by authorized guides.

Chapter 4: Yellowstone's Natural Wonders

A. The Geothermal Features

Welcome to Yellowstone National Park, a place where the Earth reveals its fiery heart. Here, the ground beneath your feet pulses with life, and the air is thick with the scent of sulfur and the promise of discovery. As you step into this geothermal wonderland, prepare to witness nature's raw power in its most mesmerizing forms.

Geysers

Imagine standing before a geyser, the ground trembling beneath you, the air thick with anticipation. Then, with a mighty roar, a column of steam and hot water erupts, reaching heights that defy belief. This is the spectacle of geysers, and Yellowstone boasts some of the world's most iconic.

- **Old Faithful**: Located in the Upper Geyser Basin, Old Faithful is the park's most famous geyser, known for its predictable eruptions approximately every 60 to 110 minutes. Witnessing its eruption is a quintessential Yellowstone experience.
- **Grand Geyser**: Also in the Upper Geyser Basin, Grand Geyser is the world's tallest predictable geyser, with eruptions that can reach up to 200 feet. Its eruptions are less frequent but longer-lasting, offering a spectacular display.
- **Steamboat Geyser**: Found in the Norris Geyser Basin, Steamboat Geyser is the world's tallest active geyser, with eruptions that can reach up to 300 feet. Its eruptions are infrequent and unpredictable, making it a rare and exciting sight when it does erupt.

Hot Springs

As you approach a hot spring, the air shimmers with heat, and the surface of the water dances with vibrant colors. These pools, heated by the Earth's internal furnace, are both beautiful and dangerous.

- **Grand Prismatic Spring**: Located in the Midway Geyser Basin, this is the largest hot spring in the United States. Its vibrant colors, ranging from deep blue to fiery red, are a result of thermophilic bacteria thriving in the varying temperatures.
- **Morning Glory Pool**: Also in the Midway Geyser Basin, this deep blue pool is known for its vivid colors and unique shape. The pool's color is due to the presence of thermophilic bacteria, and its shape resembles a morning glory flower.
- **Norris Geyser Basin**: This basin is home to the hottest and most acidic waters in the park. The area features a variety of geothermal features, including fumaroles, hot springs, and geysers.

Mudpots and Fumaroles

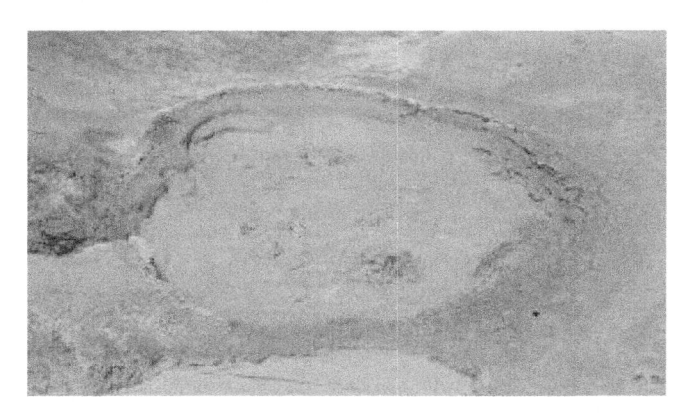

In certain areas, the ground bubbles and steams, releasing sulfurous gases that fill the air with a pungent aroma. These features, though less visually striking, offer a glimpse into the Earth's dynamic processes.

- **Mud Volcano Area**: Located in the Hayden Valley, this area features a variety of geothermal features, including mud pots, fumaroles, and hot springs. The area is known for its sulfuric smell and the Dragon's Mouth Spring, a cave-like feature that emits steam and gas.
- **Artists' Paintpots**: Situated in the Lower Geyser Basin, this area is known for its colorful hot springs and thermal mud pots. The mud pots are acidic hot springs that contain microorganisms that decompose the rock in their environment, creating mud as the limited amount of surrounding water bubbles.

B. Iconic Geothermal Sites

Yellowstone National Park is a realm where the Earth's raw energy manifests in spectacular forms. As you journey through this geothermal wonderland, you'll encounter sites that not only captivate the eye but also stir the soul. Let's explore some of the park's most iconic geothermal features.

1. Old Faithful Geyser

Location: Upper Geyser Basin, Yellowstone National Park, Wyoming.

Description: Old Faithful is perhaps the most renowned geyser in the world, celebrated for its predictable eruptions. These eruptions, which can reach heights of up to 180 feet, occur approximately every 60 to 110 minutes, offering visitors a reliable spectacle of nature's power. The geyser's name, "Old Faithful," reflects its consistent behavior, making it a must-see attraction for anyone visiting the park.

How to Reach: Accessible via the main park road, the geyser is a short walk from the Old Faithful Visitor Education Center, where you can find information on eruption times and safety guidelines.

Activities: Witnessing an eruption is the highlight. The area also offers boardwalks that allow you to explore other geothermal features in the vicinity.

Accommodations: The historic Old Faithful Inn, located nearby, offers rustic charm and modern amenities. Reservations are highly recommended, especially during peak seasons.

Dining: The Old Faithful Inn Dining Room provides a range of meals with views of the geyser. For a quicker bite, the Bear Paw Deli offers sandwiches and snacks.

Best Time to Visit: Late spring to early fall (May to September) offers the most accessible conditions. However, each season presents unique experiences, from vibrant wildflowers in spring to snow-capped landscapes in winter.

Booking: For accommodations and dining reservations, visit the official Yellowstone National Park Lodges website.

Website: Yellowstone National Park Lodges

2.Grand Prismatic Spring

Location: Midway Geyser Basin, Yellowstone National Park, Wyoming.

Description: The Grand Prismatic Spring is the largest hot spring in the United States and the third-largest in the world. Its vibrant colors, ranging from deep blue to fiery red, are a result of thermophilic bacteria thriving in the varying temperatures. The vivid hues and immense size make it one of the most photographed features in the park.

How to Reach: Accessible via the main park road, the spring is a short walk from the Grand Prismatic Spring Overlook Trail, which offers a panoramic view of the spring.

Activities: Explore the boardwalks around the spring, but maintain a safe distance from the water. The nearby Fairy Falls Trail provides an elevated view of the spring from the overlook.

Accommodations: The nearest accommodations are in the Old Faithful area, approximately 10 miles away. For a more rustic experience, consider the Madison Campground, which is closer to the Midway Geyser Basin.

Dining: Dining options are limited near the Midway Geyser Basin. It's advisable to bring snacks and water, especially if planning to hike the nearby trails.

Best Time to Visit: Late spring to early fall (May to September) offers the most accessible conditions. However, each season presents unique experiences, from vibrant wildflowers in spring to snow-capped landscapes in winter.

Booking: For accommodations and dining reservations, visit the official Yellowstone National Park Lodges website.

Website: Yellowstone National Park Lodges

Mammoth Hot Springs

Location: Mammoth Hot Springs Historic District, Yellowstone National Park, Wyoming.

Description: Mammoth Hot Springs is a large complex of hot springs on a hill of travertine in Yellowstone National Park adjacent to Fort Yellowstone and the Mammoth Hot Springs Historic District. It was created over thousands of years as hot water from the spring cooled and deposited calcium carbonate. The terraces have been deposited by the spring over many years but, due to recent minor earthquake activity, the spring vent has shifted, rendering the terraces dry.

How to Reach: Accessible via the main park road, the springs are a short walk from the Mammoth Hot Springs Hotel.

Activities: Explore the boardwalks that wind through the travertine terraces, offering close-up views of the mineral deposits. The area also features the historic Fort Yellowstone and the Albright Visitor Center.

Accommodations: The Mammoth Hot Springs Hotel offers historic charm with modern amenities. Reservations are recommended, especially during peak seasons.

Dining: The Mammoth Hot Springs Hotel Dining Room provides a range of meals with views of the terraces. For a quicker bite, the Mammoth Hot Springs Hotel Grill offers sandwiches and snacks.

Best Time to Visit: Late spring to early fall (May to September) offers the most accessible conditions. However, each season presents unique experiences, from wildflowers in spring to snow-capped landscapes in winter.

Booking: For accommodations and dining reservations, visit the official Yellowstone National Park Lodges website.

Website: Yellowstone National Park Lodges

<u>Safety and Preservation</u>

As you explore these geothermal wonders, remember that they are fragile and dangerous. The ground can be thin, and the waters are scalding hot. Always stay on designated paths and boardwalks, and never touch or throw objects into the features. Your safety and the preservation of these natural wonders depend on your respect and caution. Remember, these geothermal sites are living, breathing parts of Yellowstone's ecosystem, and they're as unpredictable as they are beautiful. Never underestimate the power of the Earth beneath you.

<u>Planning Your Visit</u>

Here are some important tips and details to make your visit to these iconic geothermal sites safe, enjoyable, and unforgettable:

- **Accommodation Options**: Staying near the geothermal sites can enhance your experience. In the Old Faithful area, **Old Faithful Inn** is a historic and charming option, offering easy access to the Upper Geyser Basin. If you prefer staying near the Grand Prismatic Spring, consider the **Madison Campground**, located nearby, or head to **Lake Yellowstone Hotel** for a scenic, lakeside experience.

- **Where to Eat**: For dining, each area offers something unique. The **Old Faithful Inn Dining Room** provides a classic dining experience with views of the geyser, while **Mammoth Hot Springs Hotel Dining Room** serves delicious meals with views of the terraces. If you're looking for something quick, **Bear Paw Deli** at Old Faithful and **Mammoth Grill** offer casual fare.
- **Cost**: Entrance to Yellowstone National Park is $35 per vehicle for a 7-day pass, which covers access to all geothermal features. For lodging and meals, prices vary depending on the time of year and type of accommodation, ranging from $100 per night for campgrounds to upwards of $350 per night for rooms at **Old Faithful Inn**.
- **Booking**: It's highly recommended to make reservations in advance, especially during the summer months. You can book accommodations, tours, and some dining options on the official **Yellowstone National Park Lodges** website or through the **Yellowstone National Park** website.
- **Safety Tips**: Always stay on marked paths and boardwalks when exploring geothermal areas. The ground can be extremely thin and unstable, and the waters in hot springs can reach temperatures that cause severe burns. Respect the park's rules, and avoid throwing objects or entering geothermal pools. Also, be mindful of wildlife in the area—keep a safe distance at all times.

C. Yellowstone Lake and Its Scenic Beauty

Located in the heart of Yellowstone National Park, Yellowstone Lake stands as a testament to nature's grandeur. Spanning 136 square miles and sitting at an elevation of 7,732 feet, it is the largest high-elevation lake in North America.

History

Formed over thousands of years, Yellowstone Lake rests within the caldera of an ancient supervolcano. This geological marvel has shaped the landscape, creating a serene body of water surrounded by majestic mountains and lush forests.

How to Reach Yellowstone Lake

Accessible via the main park roads, Yellowstone Lake is a short drive from popular entrances like the South Entrance and the East Entrance. The lake's shoreline is dotted with scenic viewpoints, picnic areas, and trailheads, making it easy to explore its beauty.

Activities to Enjoy

- **Boating and Fishing**: The lake offers opportunities for boating and fishing. Guided fishing tours are available, providing equipment and expertise to enhance your experience.
- **Hiking**: Several trails wind along the lake's shoreline, offering breathtaking views and chances to observe local wildlife. The **Storm Point Trail** is a popular choice, providing panoramic vistas of the lake and surrounding areas.
- **Wildlife Viewing**: The area around Yellowstone Lake is rich in wildlife. Early mornings and late afternoons are ideal times to spot animals such as bison, elk, and various bird species.

Where to Stay

- **Grant Village**: Located on the lake's western shore, Grant Village offers lodging options, a marina, and dining facilities. It's a convenient base for exploring the lake and nearby attractions.
- **Fishing Bridge RV Park**: Situated near the lake's eastern shore, this RV park provides full-hookup sites and is close to the Fishing Bridge Visitor Center.

Dining Options

- **Grant Village Dining Room**: Overlooking the lake, this restaurant offers a variety of American cuisine, including fresh fish and local specialties.

- **Lake Lodge Cafeteria**: For a more casual dining experience, the cafeteria provides quick meals with views of the lake.

Best Time to Visit

The ideal time to visit Yellowstone Lake is during the summer months, from June to September, when the weather is warm and most facilities are open. However, each season offers unique experiences:

- **Spring (May-June)**: Witness the park's flora awakening, with wildflowers blooming and wildlife actively foraging.
- **Fall (September-October)**: Enjoy cooler temperatures and vibrant autumn colors, with fewer crowds.
- **Winter (November-April)**: Experience a serene, snow-covered landscape, ideal for cross-country skiing and snowshoeing.

Booking Information

Reservations for accommodations, guided tours, and dining can be made through the official Yellowstone National Park Lodges website. It's advisable to book well in advance, especially during peak seasons, to secure your preferred options.

Safety Tips

- **Wildlife Safety**: Maintain a safe distance from all wildlife. Use binoculars for a closer view and never approach or feed animals.
- **Water Safety**: While the lake is beautiful, swimming is not recommended due to cold temperatures and strong currents.

- **Weather Preparedness**: Weather in Yellowstone can be unpredictable. Dress in layers and carry rain gear, even during summer months.

Additional Information

- **Fishing Regulations**: Fishing is permitted in Yellowstone Lake, but it's essential to obtain a valid fishing permit and adhere to park regulations to protect the ecosystem.
- **Accessibility**: Many areas around the lake are accessible to visitors with mobility challenges. Check the National Park Service website for detailed information on accessible facilities and trails.

D. Yellowstone's Rivers and Waterfalls

Yellowstone National Park is a sanctuary where the Earth's natural beauty unfolds in breathtaking displays.

Among its most captivating features are the rivers and waterfalls that carve through the landscape, each telling a story of geological wonder and timeless allure.

Yellowstone River and the Grand Canyon of the Yellowstone

The Yellowstone River, the longest undammed river in the contiguous United States, meanders through the park, shaping the iconic Grand Canyon of the Yellowstone. This majestic canyon, with its vibrant hues and towering cliffs, is a testament to the river's erosive power over millennia.

- **Lower Falls**: At 308 feet, the Lower Falls is the park's most famous waterfall, cascading into the canyon below. The view from Artist's Point is particularly stunning, offering a classic perspective of the falls framed by the canyon's colorful walls.
- **Upper Falls**: Less visited but equally impressive, the Upper Falls plunges 109 feet into the canyon. The Brink of the Upper Falls Trail provides a close-up view, allowing you to feel the mist and hear the roar of the water.

Tower Fall

Located near the Tower-Roosevelt area, Tower Fall is a picturesque 132-foot waterfall framed by unique rock formations. A short, paved trail leads to a viewing platform, offering a perfect spot for photography.

Gibbon Falls

Situated along the road between Madison and Norris Junctions, Gibbon Falls is a 84-foot cascade that tumbles over a wide, rocky ledge. A pullout area provides a convenient stop to admire the falls and the surrounding scenery.

Lewis Falls

Found near the South Entrance, Lewis Falls is a 29-foot waterfall on the Lewis River. A short, easy trail leads to a viewing area, making it accessible for all visitors.

Bechler River and Its Cascades

In the park's remote southwest corner, the Bechler River, known as "Cascade Corner," features numerous waterfalls and cascades. Notable falls include Dunanda Falls, a 150-foot cascade, and Ouzel Falls, a 230-foot drop. Accessing this area requires a backcountry hike, offering a more secluded experience.

Safety and Preservation

While exploring these natural wonders, it's crucial to prioritize safety and environmental stewardship:

- **Stay on Designated Trails**: Many waterfalls are best viewed from established viewpoints or trails. Venturing off-path can be dangerous and may damage delicate ecosystems.
- **Wildlife Awareness**: Always maintain a safe distance from wildlife. Remember, you are in their habitat.
- **Leave No Trace**: Pack out all trash, stay on designated paths, and avoid disturbing natural features.

Planning Your Visit

- **Best Time to Visit**: Late spring to early fall (May to September) offers the most accessible conditions. However, each season presents unique experiences, from vibrant wildflowers in spring to snow-capped landscapes in winter.
- **Accommodations**: Options range from rustic lodges like the Old Faithful Inn to campgrounds and nearby hotels in gateway towns such as West Yellowstone and Gardiner. Booking well in advance is recommended, especially during peak seasons.
- **Guided Tours**: For a deeper understanding, consider guided tours that offer insights into the park's geology, wildlife, and history. Many tour operators provide day trips focusing on specific areas or themes.

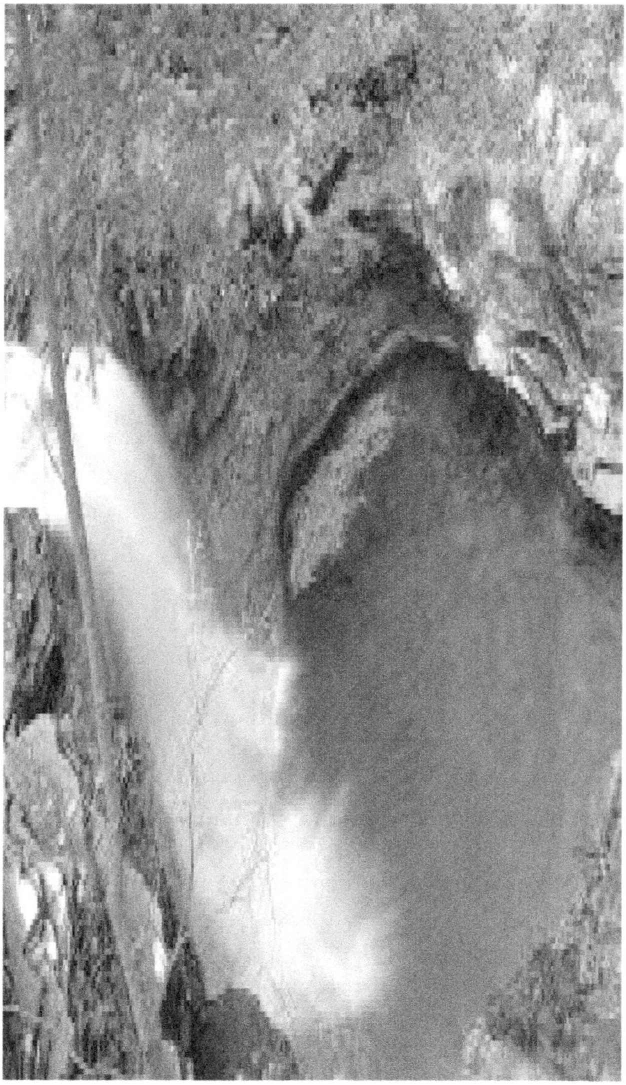

Chapter 5: Outdoor Activities

A. Hiking Trails for all Levels

Yellowstone National Park offers a diverse array of hiking trails, each providing unique experiences that cater to hikers of all skill levels. Whether you're a seasoned adventurer or a family with young children, there's a trail that awaits your exploration.

Easy Hikes: Perfect for Beginners and Families

1. **Riverside Trail**
    - **Distance**: 1.5 miles (one-way)
    - **Trail Type**: Out-and-back
    - **Highlights**: This serene, flat trail follows the Madison River, offering opportunities to spot wildlife such as elk and bison along the riverbanks.
    - **Location**: Near the West Entrance of the park.

- Difficulty: Easy
2. **West Thumb Geyser Basin**
    - **Distance**: 1-mile loop
    - **Trail Type**: Loop
    - **Highlights**: Explore geothermal features like bubbling pools and steaming fumaroles along the edge of Yellowstone Lake.
    - **Location**: Along the Grand Loop Road, near the West Thumb Junction.
    - **Difficulty**: Easy
3. **Fountain Paint Pot Trail**
    - **Distance**: 0.5 miles (round trip)
    - **Trail Type**: Boardwalk
    - **Highlights**: Witness mud pots, geysers, and hot springs in this geothermal area.
    - **Location**: Near the Midway Geyser Basin, accessible via the Fountain Flats Drive.
    - **Difficulty**: Easy

Moderate Hikes: For the Casual Adventurer

1. **Fairy Falls Trail**
    - **Distance**: 5 miles (round trip)
    - **Trail Type**: Out-and-back
    - **Highlights**: A gentle hike leading to a stunning 200-foot waterfall, with views of the Grand Prismatic Spring along the way.
    - **Location**: Near the Midway Geyser Basin, accessible via the Fairy Falls Trailhead.
    - **Difficulty**: Moderate
2. **Lamar River Trail**
    - **Distance**: 5 miles (round trip)

- **Trail Type**: Out-and-back
- **Highlights**: Offers opportunities to see wildlife like bison and wolves, especially in the early morning or late evening.
- **Location**: Near the Northeast Entrance, accessible via the Lamar Valley.
- **Difficulty**: Moderate

Safety Tips

- **Wildlife Safety**: Always maintain a safe distance from wildlife. Use binoculars for a closer view and never approach or feed animals.
- **Trail Conditions**: Check current trail conditions and weather forecasts before heading out. Some trails may be closed seasonally or due to weather conditions.
- **Preparation**: Carry sufficient water, wear appropriate footwear, and bring a map or GPS device. Cell service may be limited in certain areas of the park.

B. Backpacking Routes and Overnight Trips

Slough Creek Trail

- **Distance**: 22 miles
- **Highlights**: Known for its scenic beauty and wildlife viewing opportunities.
- **Trail Type**: Out-and-back
- **Location**: Slough Creek Campground.
- **Difficulty**: Moderate

Sepulcher Mountain Trail

- **Distance**: Varies, with several options to extend
- **Highlights**: Offering panoramic views of the park's diverse landscapes.
- **Trail Type**: Out-and-back
- **Location**: Near Tower Junction.
- **Difficulty**: Challenging

Yellowstone River Trail (Black Canyon)

- **Distance**: Varies
- **Highlights**: Parallels the north shore of the Yellowstone River, offering breathtaking canyon views.
- **Trail Type**: Out-and-back
- **Location**: Between Gardiner and Tower Junction.
- **Difficulty**: Moderate to difficult

Shoshone Lake Trail

- **Distance**: Varies, one of the longer backcountry options
- **Highlights**: Trail leads to the southwest shore of Shoshone Lake and Shoshone Geyser Basin.
- **Trail Type**: Out-and-back
- **Location**: Southwest corner of Yellowstone, access via the West Thumb area.
- **Difficulty**: Moderate to difficult

Permits and Regulations

- **Backcountry Permits**: All overnight stays in Yellowstone's backcountry require a permit, which can be obtained online or at park visitor centers. It's highly recommended to secure

permits in advance, especially during peak seasons.
- **Guided Trips**: For those who prefer a guided experience, several companies offer overnight backpacking trips, including options like llama packing and horseback riding, which include necessary permits and provide expert guidance. Website:Yellowstone Commercial Guided Trips

C. Boating, Fishing, and Water Sports

Boating in Yellowstone

- **Yellowstone Lake**: As the largest body of water in the park, Yellowstone Lake spans 136 square miles and offers breathtaking views. Boating is permitted on the lake, with options for both motorized and non-motorized vessels. A valid boat inspection and permit are required before launching.
- **Lewis Lake**: Located near the South Entrance, Lewis Lake allows motorized boating. It's a popular spot for fishing and offers scenic views of the surrounding mountains.
- **Shoshone Lake**: Accessible only by hand-powered boats, Shoshone Lake is the largest backcountry lake in the park. The lake is known for its fishing opportunities and the nearby Shoshone Geyser Basin.

Fishing in Yellowstone

- **Yellowstone Lake**: Home to native Cutthroat Trout and non-native Lake Trout, the lake offers

excellent fishing opportunities. Anglers can charter guided boats for fishing trips, with options for both fishing and sightseeing. Website: yellowstonenationalparklodges.com
- **Lewis Lake**: Known for its brown and lake trout populations, Lewis Lake is a favorite among anglers. Fishing is permitted from boats, and a valid fishing permit is required.
- **Yellowstone River**: Considered one of the greatest trout streams, the river offers fishing opportunities for brown, rainbow, and native Yellowstone cutthroat trout. The river is accessible for fishing from various points within the park.

Water Sports and Activities

- **Rafting and Kayaking**: While swimming is not permitted in most of the park's waters due to cold temperatures and strong currents, kayaking and canoeing are popular on certain lakes. It's essential to check current regulations and conditions before embarking on water activities. Website: yellowstonepark.com
- **Guided Tours**: For those interested in exploring the park's waterways without the need for personal equipment, guided boat tours are available. These tours offer insights into the park's history, geology, and wildlife, all while navigating its scenic lakes and rivers.

Planning Your Water Adventure

- **Permits and Regulations**: All watercraft must have a Yellowstone boat permit and undergo an Aquatic Invasive Species (AIS) inspection before launching. Fishing requires a valid

Yellowstone National Park fishing permit. Detailed information on permits and regulations can be found on the National Park Service's official website.
- **Safety**: Always wear a life jacket when on the water, regardless of the type of vessel. Be aware of weather conditions, as they can change rapidly in the park. Stay informed about current conditions and any advisories.
- **Best Time to Visit**: The summer months, from June through September, offer the most favorable conditions for water activities. However, always check current conditions and any advisories before planning your trip.

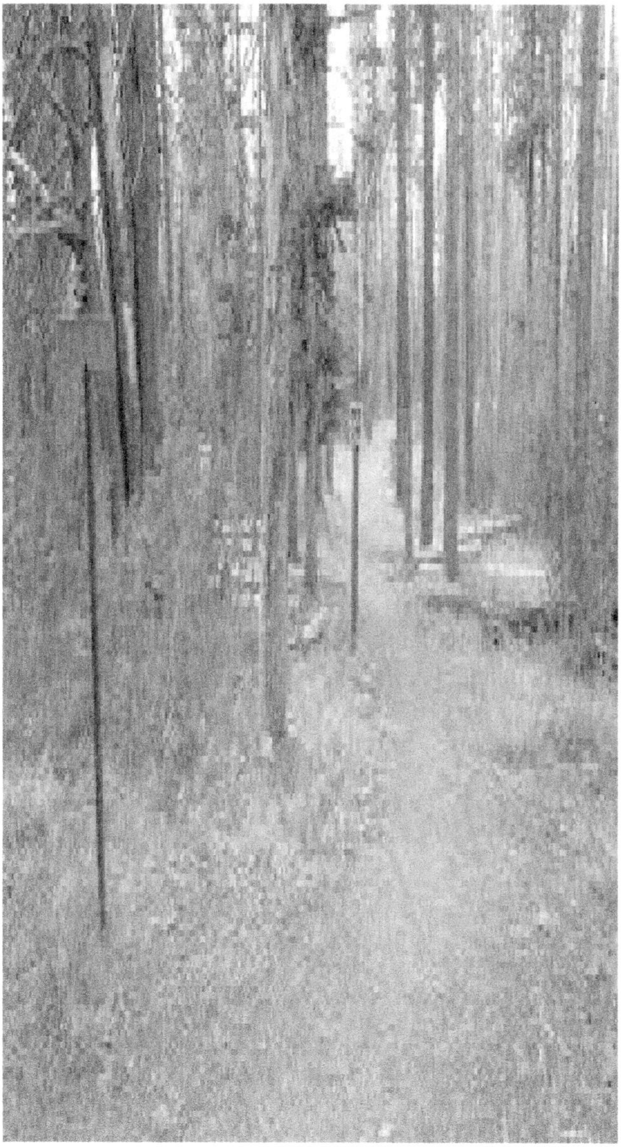

Chapter 6: Wildlife Encounters

Yellowstone National Park is a sanctuary for diverse wildlife, offering visitors the chance to observe animals in their natural habitats. To enhance your experience, it's essential to understand the park's "Big Five," the best locations for wildlife viewing, safe observation practices, and opportunities for bird watching.

A. The Big Five

Yellowstone's "Big Five" refers to the park's most iconic and sought-after wildlife species:

1. **Bison**: As the largest land mammals in North America, bison are a symbol of the park's wilderness. They can often be seen grazing in meadows and along roadsides.
2. **Elk**: Recognizable by their impressive antlers, elk are abundant in Yellowstone. During the fall

rut, their distinctive bugling calls echo through the valleys.
3. **Grizzly Bears**: These formidable creatures roam the park's forests and meadows. While sightings are less frequent, they are a highlight for many visitors.
4. **Gray Wolves**: Reintroduced to the park in the 1990s, gray wolves have established a strong presence. Observing them in the wild is a rare and thrilling experience.
5. **Moose**: With their distinctive long legs and large, broad faces, moose are often found near water sources, especially during dawn and dusk.

B. Best Places for Wildlife Viewing

To increase your chances of encountering these magnificent animals, consider visiting the following areas:

- **Lamar Valley**: Often dubbed the "Serengeti of North America," this expansive valley is teeming with wildlife, including bison, elk, black bears, grizzly bears, and wolves. Accessible via Highway 212, it's a prime spot for early morning and late afternoon viewing.
- **Hayden Valley**: This large valley is home to a variety of animals, including bison, elk, grizzly bears, and wolves. The valley is also home to Yellowstone Lake, which is a great spot for bird watching
- **Mammoth Hot Springs**: A unique habitat where elk and bison often mingle, especially during the winter months. The area also offers opportunities to see ospreys and bald eagles.

C. How to Safely Observe Wildlife

While the allure of close encounters with wildlife is strong, safety is paramount:

- **Maintain a Safe Distance**: Always stay at least 100 yards (91 meters) away from bears and wolves, and 25 yards (23 meters) from all other wildlife.
- **Use Binoculars and Telephoto Lenses**: These tools allow for close-up views without approaching the animals.
- **Stay in Your Vehicle**: When possible, observe wildlife from the safety of your car.
- **Avoid Feeding Animals**: Feeding wildlife can alter their natural behaviors and may be dangerous.
- **Stay Alert**: Be aware of your surroundings, especially during dawn and dusk when animals are most active.

D. Bird Watching in Yellowstone

Yellowstone is a haven for bird enthusiasts, with over 300 species documented within the park. Notable species include bald eagles, trumpeter swans, common loons, ospreys, American white pelicans, and sandhill cranes.

Top Birding Hotspots:

- **Pelican Creek and Yellowstone River**: Wetland areas along these waterways are excellent for spotting wading birds such as herons and egrets.
- **Lake Butte Overlook**: Offers panoramic views of Yellowstone Lake and the surrounding mountains, making it a prime spot for observing various bird species.
- **Mammoth Hot Springs**: The unique landscape attracts a variety of bird species, including ospreys and bald eagles.

Best Time for Bird Watching:

- **Spring (May to June)**: Migratory birds are abundant, and the park's wetlands are teeming with activity.
- **Fall (September to October)**: Many species are preparing for migration, offering opportunities to observe a variety of birds.

Additional Tips:

- **Bring a Field Guide**: A birding guide specific to Yellowstone can enhance your experience.
- **Join Guided Tours**: Local experts can provide valuable insights and increase your chances of sightings.
- **Dress Appropriately**: Layered clothing and waterproof gear are essential for comfort during early morning excursions.

Chapter 7: Where to Stay in Yellowstone

A. Lodgings Inside The Park

1. Old Faithful Inn

- **Location:** Upper Geyser Basin, near Old Faithful Geyser.
- **Description:** As the largest log structure in the world, this historic inn provides a rustic yet comfortable experience. Its central location allows easy access to the iconic Old Faithful Geyser.
- **Accommodations:** Offers hotel rooms and cabins.
- **Season:** Open from late May through early October.
- **Rates:** Starting at approximately $164 per night.

2. Lake Yellowstone Hotel and Cabins

- **Location:** Along the shores of Yellowstone Lake.
- **Description:** This elegant hotel combines classic architecture with modern amenities, offering stunning lake views.
- **Accommodations:** Features hotel rooms and cabins.
- **Season:** Open from mid-May to early October.
- **Rates:** Starting at around $340 per night.

3. Canyon Lodge and Cabins

- **Location:** Near the Grand Canyon of Yellowstone.
- **Description:** The largest lodging facility in the park, offering a variety of accommodations.
- **Accommodations:** Includes hotel rooms and cabins.
- **Season:** Open from late May through early October.
- **Rates:** Starting at approximately $255 per night.

4. Grant Village Lodge

- **Location:** On the southwest shore of Yellowstone Lake.
- **Description:** A peaceful retreat offering comfortable accommodations with easy access to the lake.
- **Accommodations:** Hotel-style rooms.
- **Season:** Open from late May through early October.
- **Rates:** Starting at around $329 per night.

5. Mammoth Hot Springs Hotel and Cabins

- **Location:** Near the park's north entrance.

- **Description:** Set amidst the park's geothermal features, this historic hotel offers a unique experience.
- **Accommodations:** Hotel rooms and cabins.
- **Season:** Open year-round.
- **Rates:** Starting at approximately $173 per night.

6. Old Faithful Snow Lodge and Cabins

- **Location:** Near Old Faithful Geyser.
- **Description:** The only lodging open during the winter months, offering a cozy retreat amidst snowy landscapes.
- **Accommodations:** Hotel rooms and cabins.
- **Season:** Open during the winter season.
- **Rates:** Starting at around $153 per night.

7. Roosevelt Lodge Cabins

- **Location:** In the Tower-Roosevelt area.
- **Description:** Experience the Old West with horseback riding and chuckwagon dinners.
- **Accommodations:** Rustic cabins.
- **Season:** Open from late May through early October.
- **Rates:** Starting at approximately $138 per night.

B. Camping In Yellowstone

1. Madison Campground

- **Location:** Near Madison Junction, where the Gibbon and Firehole Rivers meet.
- **Season:** Early May to mid-October.

- **Amenities:** Flush toilets, cell reception, firewood for sale, two free showers per night, and a dump station.
- **RV Information:** Some sites accommodate rigs up to 40 feet; no hookups available.
- **Reservations:** Required; book through Yellowstone National Park Lodges.

2. Bridge Bay Campground

- **Location:** Near Yellowstone Lake.
- **Season:** Mid-May to early September.
- **Amenities:** Flush toilets, cell reception, firewood for sale, two free showers per night, and a dump station.
- **RV Information:** Some sites fit rigs up to 40 feet; no hookups.
- **Reservations:** Required; book through Yellowstone National Park Lodges.

3. Canyon Campground

- **Location:** Near the Grand Canyon of Yellowstone.
- **Season:** Mid-June to early September.
- **Amenities:** Flush toilets, cell reception, firewood for sale, two free showers per night, and a dump station.
- **RV Information:** Some sites accommodate rigs up to 40 feet; no hookups.
- **Reservations:** Required; book through Yellowstone National Park Lodges.

4. Fishing Bridge RV Park

- **Location:** Near Yellowstone Lake.
- **Season:** Mid-May to early September.

- **Amenities:** Full hookups (water, sewer, and electrical), laundry facilities, showers, and a dump station.
- **RV Information:** Hard-sided vehicles only; no tents or tent-trailers.
- **Reservations:** Required; book through Yellowstone National Park Lodges.

5. Mammoth Campground

- **Location:** Near the park's north entrance.
- **Season:** Open year-round.
- **Amenities:** Flush toilets, cell reception, firewood for sale, and a dump station.
- **RV Information:** Some sites accommodate rigs up to 30 feet; no hookups.
- **Reservations:** Required; book through Yellowstone National Park Lodges.

General Tips:

- **Reservations:** Due to high demand, especially during peak seasons, it's advisable to book well in advance.
- **Amenities:** While staying inside the park offers convenience, amenities may be more limited compared to accommodations outside the park.
- **Cell Service and Wi-Fi:** Expect limited or no cell service and Wi-Fi in many areas within the park.
- **Wildlife:** Always maintain a safe distance from wildlife and follow park guidelines.

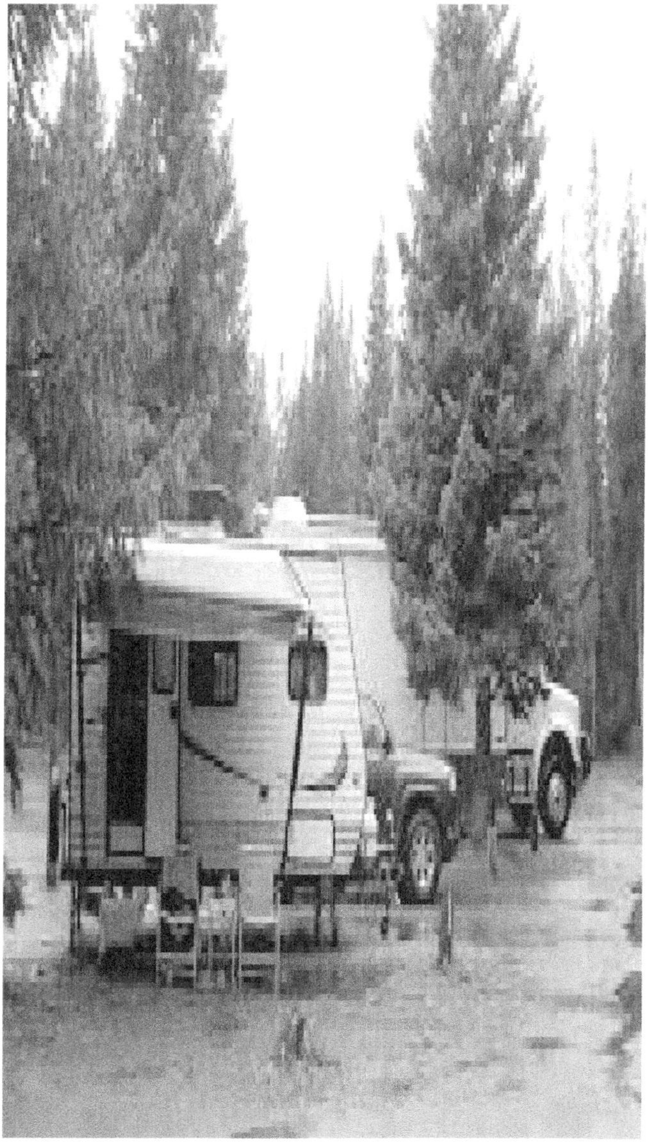

Chapter 8: Dining and Shopping

A. Best Restaurants and Dining Spots in the Park

1. Old Faithful Inn Dining Room

- **Location:** Upper Geyser Basin, near Old Faithful Geyser
- **Description:** The historic Old Faithful Inn is one of Yellowstone's most iconic buildings, offering an elegant yet cozy dining experience. The restaurant features a beautiful grand log structure with soaring ceilings and floor-to-ceiling windows, giving diners stunning views of the geyser basin.
- **Cuisine:** American fare with a focus on regional and local ingredients such as bison, trout, and local vegetables.

- **Must-Try:** Bison burgers, pan-seared trout, huckleberry pie, and homemade bread.
- **Cost:** Expect to pay $20-$40 per person, depending on your meal choices.
- **Opening Hours:** Open daily from 7:00 AM to 9:00 PM (seasonal, typically late May to early October).
- **Reservations:** Highly recommended, especially during peak seasons. Book through Yellowstone National Park Lodges.

2. Lake Yellowstone Hotel Dining Room

- **Location:** Along the shores of Yellowstone Lake
- **Description:** This elegant and historic hotel offers upscale dining with breathtaking views of Yellowstone Lake. With its refined ambiance and classic architecture, the dining room provides a fine dining experience that's perfect for a special night out.
- **Cuisine:** Upscale American cuisine with an emphasis on fresh, seasonal, and local ingredients. Dishes include pan-seared trout, bison steak, and locally sourced salads.
- **Must-Try:** Pan-seared trout, wild game dishes, and the signature huckleberry cheesecake.
- **Cost:** Entrees range from $25 to $50 per person.
- **Opening Hours:** Open daily for dinner from 5:30 PM to 9:00 PM (seasonal, typically mid-May to early October).
- **Reservations:** Strongly recommended, especially in the summer.

3. Canyon Lodge Dining Room

- **Location:** Near the Grand Canyon of the Yellowstone
- **Description:** The Canyon Lodge Dining Room offers a comfortable and casual dining experience with a beautiful view of the surrounding landscape. It's perfect for families and groups, offering a range of menu options from hearty breakfasts to satisfying dinners.
- **Cuisine:** A mix of American comfort food with a focus on fresh, hearty meals. Options include salads, sandwiches, and grilled meats.
- **Must-Try:** Steak, fresh salads, and the daily chef's special.
- **Cost:** Most meals range from $12 to $30 per person.
- **Opening Hours:** Breakfast from 7:00 AM to 9:00 AM, lunch from 11:30 AM to 2:30 PM, and dinner from 5:00 PM to 9:00 PM (seasonal, typically late May to early October).
- **Reservations:** Not required, but suggested during busy times.

4. Mammoth Hot Springs Dining Room

- **Location:** Near Mammoth Hot Springs
- **Description:** Located in the park's northern section, this casual dining room serves hearty meals in a laid-back atmosphere. The restaurant is a great place to enjoy a meal after exploring the hot springs or hiking nearby trails.
- **Cuisine:** Traditional American comfort food with some regional specialties like elk and bison.
- **Must-Try:** Elk meatloaf, homemade bread, and fresh salads.
- **Cost:** Prices range from $15 to $30 per person.

- **Opening Hours:** Open daily from 6:00 AM to 9:00 PM (seasonal, typically year-round).
- **Reservations:** Recommended for dinner, especially during peak months.

5. Obsidian Dining Room (at the Old Faithful Snow Lodge)

- **Location:** Near Old Faithful Geyser
- **Description:** Located inside the Old Faithful Snow Lodge, this dining room offers a warm and cozy atmosphere, ideal for a hearty meal after a day of skiing or winter exploration. The lodge offers a mix of casual and more upscale options, with an emphasis on fresh, local ingredients.
- **Cuisine:** American and comfort food, including steaks, burgers, and bison.
- **Must-Try:** Bison steak, huckleberry milkshakes, and the signature baked goods.
- **Cost:** Expect to spend $18 to $40 per person.
- **Opening Hours:** Open daily from 7:00 AM to 9:00 PM (seasonal, typically mid-December to early March for winter, and late May to October for summer).
- **Reservations:** Reservations are suggested, especially during the winter season.

6. The Roosevelt Lodge Dining Room

- **Location:** Tower-Roosevelt area, near the park's northern section
- **Description:** For an Old West experience, head to Roosevelt Lodge, where guests can enjoy a rustic and authentic atmosphere. The lodge offers a chuckwagon-style dinner with a campfire ambiance.

- **Cuisine:** Western-inspired dishes, including slow-cooked meats, potatoes, and vegetables.
- **Must-Try:** Slow-cooked bison stew, chuckwagon dinner, and wild game specialties.
- **Cost:** Approximately $20 to $35 per person for a full dinner.
- **Opening Hours:** Breakfast from 7:30 AM to 9:00 AM, dinner from 5:30 PM to 9:00 PM (seasonal, typically late May to early October).
- **Reservations:** Required for the chuckwagon dinner.

Additional Dining Tips:

- **Cafeterias & Quick Eats:**
  For those on the go, Yellowstone offers a variety of quick-service options at locations like the **Lake Lodge Cafeteria**, **Canyon Cafeteria**, and **Mammoth Hot Springs Cafeteria**. These are perfect for grabbing a quick bite or a picnic lunch to enjoy while exploring the park.
- **Food Trucks & Seasonal Stands:**
  During the summer months, food trucks and seasonal stands pop up at popular areas like **Old Faithful**, **Mammoth**, and **Grant Village**. These offer casual bites such as ice cream, hot dogs, and snacks. Perfect for a quick refreshment during your adventures.

B. Picnic Areas and Outdoor Dining

Yellowstone National Park also offers several beautiful picnic areas where you can enjoy a more laid-back dining experience. These spots are perfect for packing your own lunch and enjoying it surrounded by nature.

1. Gibbon Falls Picnic Area

- **Location:** Near Gibbon Falls
- **Description:** With scenic views of Gibbon Falls, this picnic area is a great place to enjoy a peaceful lunch in the park. It features shaded tables and plenty of space for spreading out.

2. Bridge Bay Picnic Area

- **Location:** Yellowstone Lake
- **Description:** Situated near the water's edge, this picnic area offers stunning lake views and is perfect for a relaxing afternoon. There are tables, restrooms, and trash disposal for convenience.

3. Grant Village Picnic Area

- **Location:** Yellowstone Lake
- **Description:** A spacious area perfect for a family picnic, offering scenic views of the lake and nearby mountains. It's close to several popular trails, so it's an ideal stop after a hike.

4. Lamar Valley Picnic Area

- **Location:** Lamar Valley
- **Description:** Known for its wildlife sightings, this picnic area offers great opportunities for both picnicking and wildlife watching. Enjoy your meal with the chance to spot bison, elk, and other animals in their natural habitat.

C. Must-Try Local Cuisine and Snacks

Yellowstone has some delicious and unique foods that should not be missed. While in the park, make sure to try these local specialties and treats:

1.Bison Burgers: Bison is a lean, flavorful meat that's popular in Yellowstone. Many of the park's restaurants feature bison burgers, often served with local toppings like caramelized onions or wild mushrooms. Try one at places like Old Faithful Inn or Canyon Lodge.

2.Trout: The waters in Yellowstone are home to wild trout, and it's a must-try dish in the park. Served grilled or pan-seared, trout is often a featured entrée at Yellowstone's fine dining restaurants. Lake Yellowstone Hotel is a great spot to try it.

3.Huckleberry Jam and Products: Huckleberries grow wild in Yellowstone and are used in everything from jams to pies and candies. Pick up some huckleberry jam as a tasty souvenir or try a huckleberry milkshake at one of the park's dining spots.

4.Elk Steaks: Another local game meat, elk, is often served as steaks or in stews. If you're looking for something truly Yellowstone, elk is a great option. Mammoth Hot Springs Dining Room is a popular spot for elk dishes.

5.Homemade Baked Goods: Many of Yellowstone's dining spots, such as the Old Faithful Inn, offer delicious homemade baked goods. From fresh pastries to pies made with locally-sourced fruits, make sure to indulge in something sweet during your visit.

D.Shopping for Souvenirs and Unique Gifts

After enjoying the natural wonders of Yellowstone, it's time to take home a memento of your trip. There are plenty of gift shops in the park that offer unique souvenirs and items that reflect the spirit of Yellowstone.

1. Old Faithful Inn Gift Shop

- **Location:** Upper Geyser Basin
- **Description:** This iconic shop inside the Old Faithful Inn offers a wide variety of souvenirs, including books on the park, locally made crafts, and Yellowstone-themed apparel. The shop's rustic vibe matches the grandeur of the Inn itself.

2. Lake Yellowstone Hotel Gift Shop

- **Location:** Yellowstone Lake
- **Description:** Located inside the historic Lake Yellowstone Hotel, this shop offers elegant souvenirs such as Yellowstone-themed jewelry, art prints, and high-quality gifts. It's perfect for picking up something special to remember your visit.

3. Mammoth Hot Springs General Store

- **Location:** Near Mammoth Hot Springs
- **Description:** This shop offers a little bit of everything, from clothing and camping gear to unique Yellowstone-themed gifts. You can find handmade crafts, home décor, and a variety of park-themed merchandise.

4. Fishing Bridge General Store

- **Location:** Yellowstone Lake
- **Description:** The perfect place to grab some last-minute souvenirs or outdoor essentials. This

store sells everything from fishing gear to Yellowstone-themed snacks and gifts.

5. Canyon Village General Store

- **Location:** Grand Canyon of the Yellowstone
- **Description:** A convenient stop for all your souvenir needs, from park maps to locally crafted jewelry and souvenirs. The shop also carries snacks and camping supplies for those continuing their adventure.

Unique Gifts to Look For:

- **Yellowstone-themed Jewelry:** Find handcrafted pieces inspired by the park's beauty, such as earrings, necklaces, and bracelets featuring wildlife motifs or iconic park symbols.
- **Local Handicrafts:** Many gift shops offer products made by local artisans, including pottery, woodwork, and woven goods.
- **Books and Art Prints:** Take home a beautiful art print of Yellowstone's landscapes or a guidebook about the park's history and wildlife.
- **Yellowstone Apparel:** From t-shirts and hats to cozy sweaters, there's a wide range of Yellowstone-branded clothing to choose from.

Chapter 9: Yellowstone Beyond the Park

A. Day Trips Near Yellowstone

Yellowstone is surrounded by several incredible natural and cultural attractions, making it an ideal base for day trips. Here's a closer look at some of the best nearby destinations, along with essential information.

1. Grand Teton National Park

- **Distance from Yellowstone:** About 60 miles south of Yellowstone
- **How to Reach:** Take US Highway 191 south from Yellowstone's south entrance, passing through Jackson Hole to Grand Teton National Park.
- **Entry Cost:** $35 per vehicle (valid for 7 days).

- **Activities:** Hiking, wildlife watching, photography, boating, and scenic drives. Don't miss a visit to Jenny Lake and the Snake River.
- **Must-See:** Jenny Lake, Snake River, Teton Glacier Trail, and the summit of Grand Teton for stunning panoramic views.
- **Website for More Info and Booking:** Grand Teton National Park
- **Tips:** Arrive early, especially in the summer, as parking and popular spots can get crowded.

2. Jackson Hole

- **Distance from Yellowstone:** About 60 miles south of Yellowstone
- **How to Reach:** From Yellowstone's south entrance, drive south along US Highway 191 for 60 miles to Jackson Hole.
- **Entry Cost:** No entry fee to visit Jackson Hole itself. Fees for specific attractions, like the National Elk Refuge or the Jackson Hole Mountain Resort, may apply.
- **Activities:** Shopping, dining, visiting art galleries, and exploring nearby wildlife refuges. You can also explore the **National Museum of Wildlife Art** or go on a wildlife safari tour.
- **Must-See:** Jackson Town Square, the National Museum of Wildlife Art, and the National Elk Refuge.
- **Website for More Info and Booking:** Jackson Hole Chamber of Commerce
- **Tips:** Jackson is known for its charming western atmosphere, so be sure to check out the local shops and restaurants for a taste of the local culture.

3. Big Sky Resort

- **Distance from Yellowstone:** About 90 miles north of Yellowstone
- **How to Reach:** From Yellowstone's West Entrance, take US Highway 191 north to Big Sky.
- **Entry Cost:** Prices vary based on the season and activities. Summer activities such as zip-lining or scenic lift rides start at around $50. Skiing rates vary by season.
- **Activities:** Ziplining, mountain biking, scenic gondola rides, hiking, and exploring the Big Sky Resort area.
- **Must-See:** Lone Peak, Ousel Falls, and the Big Sky Resort village.
- **Website for More Info and Booking:** Big Sky Resort
- **Tips:** If you're visiting in summer, the resort offers a range of outdoor activities, from hiking to mountain biking and guided tours.

4. Lewis and Clark Caverns State Park

- **Distance from Yellowstone:** About 150 miles northeast of Yellowstone
- **How to Reach:** Drive east from Yellowstone to the town of Livingston, then head northeast to the caverns via MT-2.
- **Entry Cost:** $12 per adult (ages 12 and over), children are free.
- **Activities:** Explore the impressive limestone caves through guided tours. The park also has hiking trails and picnic areas.
- **Must-See:** The extensive limestone formations inside the cave.

- **Website for More Info and Booking:** Lewis and Clark Caverns State Park
- **Tips:** Tours are popular in summer, so consider reserving tickets in advance. Be prepared for a steep climb to the caves.

5. Cody, Wyoming

- **Distance from Yellowstone:** About 50 miles east of Yellowstone
- **How to Reach:** From Yellowstone's East Entrance, take US-14/16/20 east to Cody.
- **Entry Cost:** Free to visit the town itself. Fees apply for certain attractions like the Buffalo Bill Center of the West, with tickets costing around $20 for adults.
- **Activities:** Explore the **Buffalo Bill Center of the West**, go to the nightly **Cody Rodeo**, and stroll through **Old Trail Town** to see preserved frontier buildings.
- **Must-See:** Buffalo Bill Center of the West, Cody Night Rodeo, and Historic Cody Mural.
- **Website for More Info and Booking:** Cody, Wyoming
- **Tips:** The Cody Rodeo, held nightly from June through August, is a fun experience for those wanting to witness authentic Western culture.

6. Shoshone National Forest

- **Distance from Yellowstone:** Just outside the park's eastern boundary
- **How to Reach:** From Yellowstone's East Entrance, head south to the Shoshone National Forest.

- **Entry Cost:** Free to access the national forest. Fees apply for camping and other activities.
- **Activities:** Hiking, fishing, camping, and exploring the scenic beauty of the forest.
- **Must-See:** Sunlight Basin, the Beartooth Mountains, and scenic drives like the **Beartooth Highway**.
- **Website for More Info:** Shoshone National Forest
- **Tips:** The Beartooth Highway offers a breathtaking scenic drive, especially in the summer when wildflowers are in bloom.

7. The Beartooth Highway

- **Distance from Yellowstone:** About 60 miles east of Yellowstone
- **How to Reach:** From Yellowstone's Northeast Entrance, drive east on US-212 to access the highway.
- **Entry Cost:** Free to drive the Beartooth Highway, though some nearby parks and scenic areas may charge an entry fee.
- **Activities:** Scenic driving, photography, and hiking. The highway is often considered one of the most beautiful in America.
- **Must-See:** Beartooth Pass and views of the Absaroka Range.
- **Website for More Info:** Beartooth Highway
- **Tips:** The Beartooth Highway is typically open from late June to October, depending on weather conditions. Be prepared for rapidly changing weather at higher elevations.

General Tips for Day Trips:

- **Plan Ahead:** For popular day trips like Grand Teton National Park or Jackson Hole, it's recommended to book activities and accommodations in advance, especially during peak seasons.
- **Pack for All Conditions:** Weather can change quickly in Yellowstone and its surrounding areas. Bring layers, sunscreen, and water to stay comfortable during your day trips.
- **Fuel Up:** Gas stations can be sparse in more remote areas like the Beartooth Highway or Shoshone National Forest. Make sure to fill up your tank before heading out.
- **Wildlife Safety:** Keep a safe distance from wildlife and be prepared to stop for animals like bison or elk, which frequently roam the roads.

B. Local Culture

1. Native American Heritage

The land around Yellowstone has been home to various Native American tribes for thousands of years. The park itself sits on lands that are historically significant to these tribes, and the surrounding areas are full of stories, traditions, and cultural sites that are worth exploring.

Must-See Spots:

- **Buffalo Bill Center of the West** – Cody, Wyoming
    - **Location:** 720 Sheridan Ave, Cody, WY
    - **Cost:** $20 for adults, $10 for children 6-17, free for children under 6.
    - **Description:** This world-class museum complex offers extensive exhibits on Native American culture, western art, and the legacy of Buffalo Bill Cody. The **Plains Indian Museum** within the center showcases Native American art, artifacts, and history, offering insights into the tribes of the Yellowstone region, including the Crow and Shoshone.
    - **Website:** Buffalo Bill Center of the West
- **Cody Night Rodeo** – Cody, Wyoming
    - **Location:** 500 W Yellowstone Ave, Cody, WY
    - **Cost:** Tickets range from $20 to $30 per person.
    - **Description:** This nightly rodeo is a must-see for anyone interested in authentic western cowboy culture. Experience thrilling rodeo events like bull riding, bronco busting, and roping. The rodeo runs from June through August and is an exciting display of traditional skills and rodeo competition.
    - **Website:** Cody Night Rodeo

- **Crow Reservation and Cultural Tours** – Near Billings, Montana
  - **Location:** Crow Agency, MT
  - **Cost:** Prices vary by tour.
  - **Description:** The Crow Tribe has a deep connection to Yellowstone and the surrounding lands. Take a guided tour of the Crow Reservation, where you can learn about their history, culture, and traditions. Some tours include visits to sacred sites, storytelling sessions, and displays of traditional arts and crafts.
  - **Website:** Crow Tribe Cultural Tours

2. Western Heritage

Yellowstone and its surrounding areas are synonymous with the American West, and the region's western heritage is deeply ingrained in the culture. The cowboy spirit is alive and well, and many towns like **Jackson** and **Cody** offer a true Wild West experience.

Iconic Western Experiences:

- **Cody Night Rodeo:** Known as the "Rodeo Capital of the World," **Cody** hosts nightly rodeos in the summer, providing a chance to experience authentic cowboy traditions and enjoy rodeo competitions such as bull riding, barrel racing, and bronco busting.
- **Historic Sites: Old Trail Town** in Cody preserves a collection of historical buildings from the frontier days, including cabins and artifacts from early settlers.
- **Western Art and Music:** Both Cody and Jackson Hole are known for their thriving arts

scenes, where local artists showcase western-inspired artwork, and galleries display sculptures, paintings, and photographs of cowboy life.

Must-See Spots:

- **Old Trail Town** – Cody, Wyoming
    - **Location:** 1831 Demaris Dr, Cody, WY
    - **Cost:** $10 for adults, $5 for children (ages 6-12).
    - **Description:** This outdoor museum in Cody offers a fascinating glimpse into the life of early settlers and frontier towns. The town features authentic log cabins, a historic church, and a blacksmith shop, all relocated from the surrounding area to preserve the early western spirit.
    - **Website:** Old Trail Town
- **National Museum of Wildlife Art** – Jackson Hole, Wyoming
    - **Location:** 2820 Runguis Rd, Jackson, WY
    - **Cost:** $18 for adults, $12 for students, free for children 12 and under.
    - **Description:** Located just outside of Jackson, this museum boasts an impressive collection of wildlife art, with over 5,000 pieces, including works by Remington, Russell, and many contemporary artists. It celebrates the animals that roamed the American West, making it a perfect stop for art lovers and wildlife enthusiasts.

- o **Website:** National Museum of Wildlife Art
- **Teton County Fair** – Jackson Hole, Wyoming
  - o **Location:** 305 W Snow King Ave, Jackson, WY
  - o **Cost:** Free entry to fairgrounds, costs for rides and events vary.
  - o **Description:** Held every summer, this county fair celebrates the local community with rodeos, carnival rides, livestock shows, and concerts. It's a great place to experience local culture, food, and entertainment in a fun, family-friendly environment.
  - o **Website:** Teton County Fair

3.Modern-Day Cowboy and Ranching Culture

Ranching is still a significant part of the culture in and around Yellowstone. Modern-day cowboys and cowgirls continue the legacy of their predecessors, and you can get a taste of ranch life through cowboy experiences and dude ranches.

Must-See Spots:

- **Triangle X Ranch** – Grand Teton National Park, Wyoming
  - o **Location:** 28 Triangle X Ranch Rd, Moose, WY
  - o **Cost:** Prices start at $125 per person for a half-day horseback ride.
  - o **Description:** This historic ranch, located in Grand Teton National Park, offers horseback riding tours through stunning mountain landscapes. You can

also stay at the ranch for a true cowboy experience, participating in cattle drives and other ranch activities.
    - **Website:** Triangle X Ranch
- **Jackson Hole Rodeo** – Jackson Hole, Wyoming
    - **Location:** 447 W Snow King Ave, Jackson, WY
    - **Cost:** $20 for general admission.
    - **Description:** Another opportunity to experience cowboy culture, the Jackson Hole Rodeo is held every Wednesday and Saturday night in the summer. Watch cowboys and cowgirls compete in bull riding, roping, and barrel racing.
    - **Website:** Jackson Hole Rodeo
- **The 7 Lazy P Ranch** – Near Jackson Hole, Wyoming
    - **Location:** 7 Lazy P Ranch, Jackson, WY
    - **Cost:** Prices for a stay range from $200 to $300 per night, depending on the season and package.
    - **Description:** Offering a quintessential dude ranch experience, this working ranch provides horseback riding, hiking, fishing, and Western-style meals. The ranch is situated in a beautiful, remote area near the Snake River and offers visitors the chance to experience life on a modern-day ranch.
    - **Website:** 7 Lazy P Ranch

4. Arts, Music, and Festivals

The cultural scene in Yellowstone's surrounding areas is lovely, with arts festivals, music performances, and art galleries celebrating the rich heritage of the region.

Must-See Spots:

- **Jackson Hole Arts Festival** – Jackson Hole, Wyoming
    - **Location:** Jackson Town Square, Jackson, WY
    - **Cost:** Varies by event.
    - **Description:** Held annually, the Jackson Hole Arts Festival brings together local and national artists for a weekend of exhibitions, performances, and workshops. It's a fantastic way to explore the local art scene and engage with artists.
    - **Website:** Jackson Hole Arts Festival
- **Cody Heritage Museum** – Cody, Wyoming
    - **Location:** 1240 9th St, Cody, WY
    - **Cost:** $10 for adults, $5 for children.
    - **Description:** This museum offers a deep dive into the cultural and historical roots of Cody, including exhibits on Native American life, the history of the town, and the life of Buffalo Bill. The museum's collections help visitors understand the unique heritage of the region.
    - **Website:** Cody Heritage Museum

C. Visiting Native American Sites and Learning About Local Tribes

Yellowstone National Park and the surrounding areas have long been inhabited by Native American tribes. These tribes have a deep connection to the land, and their history and culture are integral to the region's identity. Exploring Native American sites and learning about local tribes offers a fascinating look at their heritage, traditions, and ongoing influence on the area.

1. The Crow Tribe (Apsáalooke)

The Crow Tribe has historically lived in the Yellowstone region, and their story is closely tied to the area's natural landscape. The Crow people, known for their skill in hunting, horseback riding, and their rich cultural traditions, continue to play an important role in the region.

Must-See Spots:

- **Crow Agency and Little Bighorn Battlefield National Monument** – Crow Agency, Montana
    - **Location:** Crow Agency, MT (near Billings, MT)
    - **Cost:** Free entry to the Crow Agency, $20 per vehicle for Little Bighorn Battlefield National Monument.
    - **Description:** While the Crow Agency itself is a working tribal center, nearby is the **Little Bighorn Battlefield**, where the Crow Tribe played a crucial role in the historic Battle of the Little Bighorn in 1876. The monument commemorates

the battle and tells the story of the Crow and Lakota Sioux tribes.
    - **Website for More Info:** Little Bighorn Battlefield
    - **Activities:** Guided tours, cultural exhibits, and exploring historical sites related to the Crow Tribe's involvement in Native American history.
- **Crow Fair** – Crow Agency, Montana
    - **Location:** Crow Fairgrounds, Crow Agency, MT
    - **Cost:** Varies depending on events.
    - **Description:** This annual event, held every August, is one of the largest Native American gatherings in the country. The Crow Fair celebrates Native American culture with rodeos, powwows, traditional dances, and arts. It's a fantastic way to experience Crow traditions, art, and hospitality.
    - **Website for More Info:** Crow Fair

2. The Shoshone Tribe

The Shoshone have lived in the Yellowstone region for centuries, and their history and culture are deeply connected to the area's rivers, forests, and wildlife. The Shoshone are known for their expertise in fishing, gathering, and their ability to thrive in the mountainous landscapes.

Must-See Spots:

- **Shoshone Tribal Lands and Cultural Center** – Fort Washakie, Wyoming

- Location: 9755 Hwy 287, Fort Washakie, WY
- Cost: Free to visit the Cultural Center; donations encouraged.
- Description: The **Shoshone Tribal Lands** include the **Wind River Indian Reservation**, where you can visit the **Shoshone Cultural Center** to learn about the tribe's history, traditional crafts, and customs. The center provides insights into the Shoshone people's deep connection to Yellowstone's wildlife and landscape.
- Website for More Info: Shoshone Tribal Lands
- Activities: Learn about Shoshone history, view traditional art, and explore exhibits about their relationship with the land.

- **Sacred Shoshone Sites** – Wind River Range, Wyoming
  - Location: Wind River Range, WY
  - Cost: Free to visit; may require permits for hiking.
  - Description: The Wind River Range is a sacred area for the Shoshone Tribe. While this area is primarily known for its incredible hiking and outdoor activities, it's also home to culturally significant sites for the Shoshone. Guided tours are available to share the tribe's historical connection to the land.
  - Activities: Hiking, wildlife watching, and cultural education tours.

3. Nez Perce Tribe

The Nez Perce Tribe's history is closely linked to the region's rivers and the landscape surrounding Yellowstone. In 1877, the tribe famously resisted U.S. Army forces in the Nez Perce War, making a remarkable retreat across several states, including Montana, before surrendering just 40 miles from the Canadian border.

Must-See Spots:

- **Nez Perce National Historic Park** – Various Locations, Idaho, Montana, and Washington
    - **Location:** Several sites, including **Spalding** and **Bear Paw Battlefield**, Montana
    - **Cost:** $5 per person, free for children under 16.
    - **Description:** The **Nez Perce National Historic Park** stretches across several states, commemorating the tribe's history, cultural heritage, and the tragic events of the Nez Perce War. The **Bear Paw Battlefield** in Montana is the site where Chief Joseph famously surrendered after a 1,170-mile retreat.
    - **Website for More Info:** Nez Perce National Historic Park
    - **Activities:** Explore historical sites, visit museums, and learn about the Nez Perce's resistance and connection to the land.

4. Yellowstone's Indigenous History

Yellowstone itself holds deep cultural significance to many Native American tribes, including the Lakota Sioux, Shoshone, Crow, and Nez Perce. These tribes considered the park's geothermal features, rivers, and wildlife as sacred. Many Native American groups used the park for hunting, gathering, and spiritual ceremonies.

Must-See Spots:

- **Yellowstone's Tribal Connections** – Various Locations in the Park
    - **Location:** Yellowstone National Park
    - **Cost:** Park entrance fee required ($35 per vehicle for a 7-day pass).
    - **Description:** While no specific "Native American site" exists within the park, several geothermal features and landmarks are of significant cultural importance to local tribes. Visitors can learn about these traditions and stories through ranger-led programs or exhibits in the park's visitor centers.
    - **Activities:** Attend ranger talks, view exhibits, and explore cultural sites like **Indian Pond** or **Yellowstone Lake**, both of which are sacred to Native Americans.
- **Indian Creek Campground and Trail** – Yellowstone National Park
    - **Location:** Located near the Lamar Valley
    - **Cost:** $20 per night for camping.
    - **Description:** This campground offers a chance to explore the cultural landscape of Yellowstone. The area is named after Native American traditions and provides access to hiking trails that lead to the **Indian Creek** area, known for its beauty and spiritual significance.

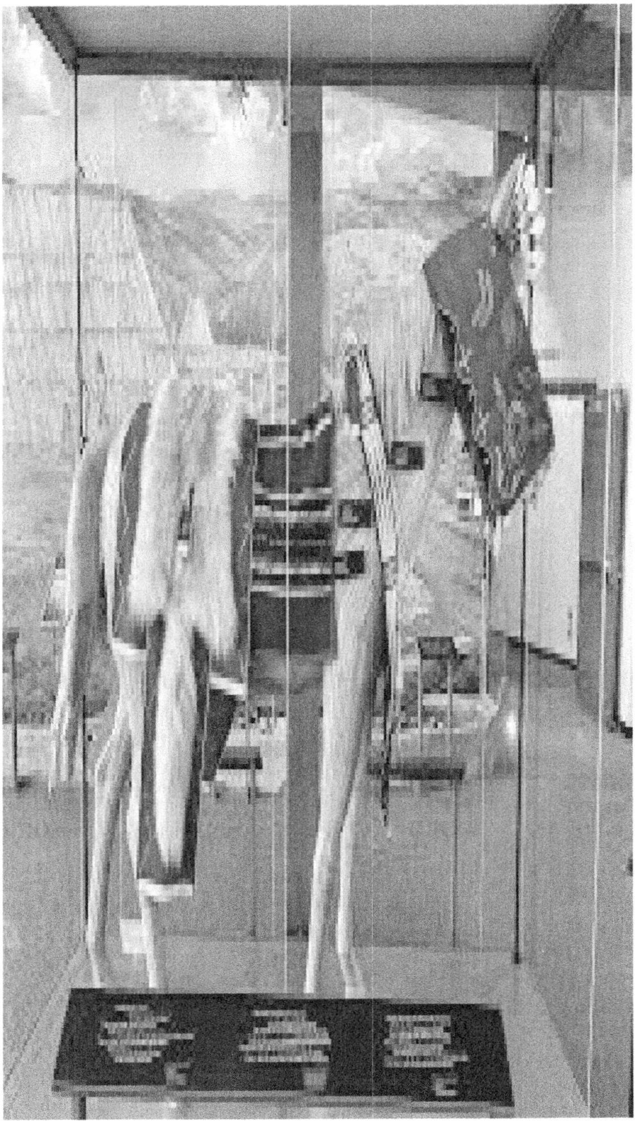

Chapter 10: Safety, Travel Tips, and Park Etiquette

A. Health and Emergency Services in the Park

Yellowstone is remote, so it's essential to know how to access health and emergency services if needed. While the park has basic medical facilities, they may not be available at all times or in all locations.

1. Medical Services

- **First-Aid Stations:** Yellowstone has a few first-aid stations and clinics. The most notable are located at **Mammoth Hot Springs** (open year-round) and **Old Faithful** (seasonal). However, these facilities are often limited to basic services.

- **Nearest Hospitals:** If you need advanced medical care, the nearest major hospitals are in **Cody, Wyoming** (about 50 miles from the East Entrance) and **Jackson, Wyoming** (about 60 miles from the South Entrance). Emergency medical airlift is available in more severe situations.

2. Emergency Contacts

- **Park Emergency Number:** If you're in immediate danger or need emergency services, dial **911** for emergency services (available in most park areas) or contact **Yellowstone Dispatch** at **307-344-7381** for non-emergency situations.

3. First-Aid Kit

- **What to Pack:** It's advisable to carry a first-aid kit with basic supplies such as bandages, antiseptic wipes, pain relievers, allergy medication, and any personal prescription medications. You may also want to carry bear spray, especially if you're hiking in bear country.

B. What to Pack for Your Yellowstone Adventure

Packing properly for your Yellowstone trip ensures that you'll be prepared for anything the park throws your way. Here's a helpful packing list:

1. Clothing

- **Layered Clothing:** Weather in Yellowstone can be unpredictable, with temperatures varying dramatically throughout the day, especially in higher elevations. Bring lightweight, moisture-wicking layers that can easily be added or removed.
- **Sturdy Footwear:** Whether you're hiking, walking around the boardwalks, or simply exploring, a good pair of hiking boots or shoes with sturdy soles is essential.
- **Rain Gear and Sunscreen:** Even if rain is unlikely, be prepared with waterproof clothing and a rain jacket. Sunscreen and a hat are crucial for protection against the high-altitude sun.

2. Essentials

- **Water Bottle:** Stay hydrated during your adventures by carrying a refillable water bottle. Many campgrounds and lodges have water stations where you can refill.
- **Binoculars and Camera:** For wildlife spotting and capturing the breathtaking scenery, binoculars and a camera are must-haves.
- **Bear Spray:** If you plan on hiking or spending time in more remote areas, bear spray is a necessary safety item.
- **Map and Guidebook:** While many areas of the park are marked, it's helpful to have a map or guidebook for trails and notable points of interest.
- **Chargers and Power Bank:** If you plan to take photos or use your phone for navigation, make sure to bring a charger and a power bank, as cell service can be limited.

C. Cell Service, Wi-Fi, and Communication While in the Park

Yellowstone's remote location means that you can expect limited or no cell service in many parts of the park. Here's what you need to know about staying connected during your visit:

1. Cell Service

- **Limited Coverage:** Cell service is available at some of the park's developed areas (like **Mammoth Hot Springs** and **Canyon Village**), but it's unreliable in more remote regions such as the Lamar Valley and the backcountry.
- **Tips:** If you need to make an important call or send a message, plan to do so when you're in an area with service, or prepare to be offline for much of your visit.

2. Wi-Fi

- **Limited Wi-Fi Access:** Wi-Fi is available at some lodges and visitor centers, but the connection may be slow or intermittent. It's best to use Wi-Fi only for essential communications or to check for park updates.
- **Visitor Centers:** Some of the larger visitor centers (like **Old Faithful Visitor Center**) offer internet access, but it's not guaranteed.

3. Communication in Emergencies

- **Satellite Phones:** If you'll be venturing into areas with no cell service, a satellite phone is a good investment for emergencies. Some guided

tours or private excursions may offer satellite phones.
- **Emergency Communication Devices:** For extended backcountry hikes, consider carrying a personal locator beacon (PLB) or satellite messenger, which can send your location to emergency services if needed.

D. Park Etiquette

Being respectful of the park's environment, wildlife, and other visitors is crucial for preserving Yellowstone's natural beauty for future generations. Here are some important etiquette tips:

1. Leave No Trace

- **Pack Out Trash:** Yellowstone is a pristine environment, and it's essential that you leave no trace. Pack out everything you bring into the park, including trash, food wrappers, and litter.
- **Stay on Trails:** Stay on designated paths and boardwalks to avoid damaging delicate ecosystems, especially around geothermal features and wildlife habitats.

2. Respect Wildlife

- **Observe from a Distance:** Keep a safe distance from wildlife. Use binoculars to get a closer look without getting too close to animals, especially bison and bears.
- **No Feeding Wildlife:** Feeding animals can harm them and disrupt their natural behavior. Never feed or approach wildlife.

3. Quiet Enjoyment

- **Respect Quiet Zones:** Yellowstone is a haven for wildlife and people seeking tranquility. Keep noise levels to a minimum, especially when hiking, camping, or exploring remote areas.

Conclusion

As we come to the end of this Yellowstone Travel Guide 2025, I want to extend my heartfelt thanks for allowing this guide to accompany you on your journey through one of the most remarkable places on Earth. Together, we've ventured through Yellowstone's expansive wilderness, explored its iconic landmarks, and uncovered the stories that make this park truly unforgettable.

We've stood in awe of the erupting geysers, marveled at the vibrant colors of hot springs, and witnessed the grace of bison and wolves in the wild. We've tasted the flavors of the park, learned about its rich Native American heritage, and connected with the land in a way that only Yellowstone can offer. Throughout this guide, my hope has been to not only provide practical insights for your visit but to inspire a deeper connection to the beauty and power of this natural wonder.

Yellowstone is not just a destination; it's an experience. It's the thrill of hearing the rumble of Old Faithful as it bursts into the sky, the joy of spotting wildlife in the Lamar Valley, and the serenity of watching the sun set over the rugged landscape. These moments remind us of the fragile beauty of the world and our deep connection to it.

As you step into Yellowstone, I encourage you to embrace its unpredictability and wild spirit. Let the park's vastness humble you and its beauty ignite your sense of adventure. Sometimes, the most meaningful moments come from the unexpected—the quiet of a secluded meadow, a chance encounter with a fellow traveler, or simply pausing to breathe in the fresh, crisp air.

Thank you for choosing this Yellowstone Travel Guide 2025 as a companion on your journey. I hope it has not only helped you plan your adventure but also deepened your love for this awe-inspiring land. Yellowstone has a way of leaving a lasting imprint on your soul, and I trust it will stay with you long after your visit.

May your travels through Yellowstone be filled with discovery, wonder, and unforgettable memories. Who knows? Perhaps our paths will cross one day as we both stand in awe of the park's beauty. Until then, happy exploring, and may the wild spirit of Yellowstone continue to guide you on all your future adventures.

Made in the USA
Coppell, TX
15 April 2025